Ladybird  Readers

The Fun Run

Series Editor: Sorrel Pitts
Story by Catherine Baker
Illustrated by Chris Jevons

Ladybird Readers Starter Level

Title		Phonics	Sight Words
1	Alphabet Book	A—Z	
2	Is it Nat?	s a t p i n	a is it
3	Nat Sits		an in sit
4	Top Dog and Pompom	m d g o c k	and can I into no
5	Top Dog is Sick		got not
6	The Fun Run	e u r h b f l	at get go has off the to up
7	Gus is Hot!		full his of on put
8	Jazz the Vet	j v w x y z qu	be but had he him she tell was
9	Vick the Vet		did well will
10	Dash and Thud	ch sh th ng	if ran then they with yes
11	Big Bad Bash		big long that this
12	The Big Fish	ai ee oa oo	her look see them
13	The Big Ship		let me my too
14	Martin and Lorna	ar or ur ow oi er	all are for
15	Farmer Carl		cut down good help now
16	The Big Dipper	igh ear air ure	as have like said some went you
17	The Silver Ring		come from so stop we what

First, go through the phonemes on page 4, and do the activity on page 5. Then, read the words in the first half of the book, focusing on pronunciation and blending.

The sight words are introduced in the second half of the book, first on their own and then in full sentences.

At the back of the book, there are activities and assessments practicing phonemes and sight words. These icons indicate the key skills required in each activity:

 Spelling and writing   Speaking   Reading

The Fun Run

Look at the story

First, look at the words and pictures.
Use the words to practice phonics.

Phonics focus

e u r h b f l

Gus

Ross

hot

Miss Less

back

fun run

Aa Bb Cc Dd Ee Ff Gg Hh Ii Jj Kk Ll Mm

Activity

1 **Look. Say the words.**
Circle the first sound. 📖 💬

1
back

g   (b)   r

2
Ross

L   F   R

3
fun run

e   f   h

4
hot

h   r   b

'n Oo Pp Qq Rr Ss Tt Uu Vv Ww Xx Yy Zz

Miss Less

Ross

Gus

fun run

fun run

back

hot

Ross

Miss Less

back

Miss Less

Ross

Gus

Ladybird Readers

The Fun Run

Read the story

Now read the story in full sentences.
Practice using the sight words.

Sight words

at

get

go

has

off

the

to

up

Gus, Ross, Mom, and Dad go to the fun run.

Gus has a lot of kit.
Ross has no kit. He is fed up.

Miss Less sets off the fun run. Mom and Dad tell Gus to run and run.

Ross is at the back.

Gus runs off, but he gets hot and he has a nap.

Ross gets hot, but he runs on.

Ross gets back to Miss Less.
Ross gets a medal.

Gus gets up.

Gus gets back, and he
gets his medal.

Activities

2 Say the words. Put a ✔ by the words with the sound *u*. 🗨 📖

1   fun run   ✔

2   Miss Less   ☐

3   hot   ☐

4   Gus   ☐

5   Ross   ☐

3 Say the sight words. Match. 🗨 📖

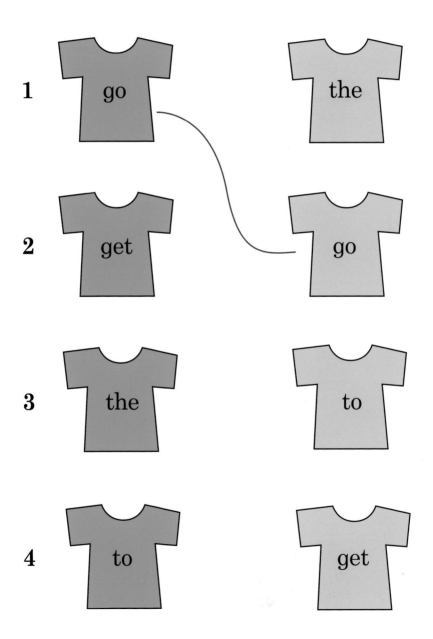

1 go   the

2 get   go

3 the   to

4 to   get

Assessment

4 Say the sounds. Write the letters.

| h | u | L | u | f | b |

1. _f_un r_u_n

2. G____s

3. ____ot

4. Miss ____ess

5. ____ack

5 Circle the correct sight words.

1 Gus, Ross, Mom, and Dad **go** / **get** to the fun run.

2 Ross is at **the** / **to** back.

3 Gus runs **at,** / **off,** but he gets hot.

4 Gus gets **has.** / **up.**

Starter

Starter 1
Alphabet Book

978–0–241–39367–3

Starter 2
Is it Nat?

978–0–241–39368–0

Starter 3
Nat Sits

978–0–241–39369–7

Starter 4
Top Dog and Pompom

978–0–241–39370–3

Starter 5
Top Dog is Sick

978–0–241–39371–0

Starter 6
The Fun Run

978–0–241–39372–7

Starter 7
Gus is Hot!

978–0–241–39373–4

Starter 8
Jazz the Vet

978–0–241–39374–1

Starter 9
Vick the Vet

978–0–241–39375–8

Starter 10
Dash and Thud

978–0–241–39376–5

Starter 11
Big Bad Bash

978–0–241–39377–2

Starter 12
The Big Fish

978–0–241–39379–6

Starter 13
The Big Ship

978–0–241–39380–2

Starter 14
Martin and Lorna

978–0–241–39381–9

Starter 15
Farmer Carl

978–0–241–39382–6

Starter 16
The Big Dipper

978–0–241–39383–3

Starter 17
The Silver Ring

978–0–241–39384–0

LADYBIRD BOOKS

UK | USA | Canada | Ireland | Australia
India | New Zealand | South Africa

Ladybird Books is part of the Penguin Random House group of companies
whose addresses can be found at global.penguinrandomhouse.com.
www.penguin.co.uk   www.puffin.co.uk   www.ladybird.co.uk

Penguin
Random House
UK

First published 2017. This edition published 2019
001

Copyright © Ladybird Books Ltd, 2017

Printed in China

A CIP catalogue record for this book is available from the British Library

ISBN: 978-0-241-39372-7

All correspondence to:
Ladybird Books
Penguin Random House Children's
80 Strand, London WC2R 0RL